EVERYBODY KNOWS A GHOST

ESSENTIAL POETS SERIES 321

Canada Council for the Arts | Conseil des Arts du Canada

ONTARIO ARTS COUNCIL
CONSEIL DES ARTS DE L'ONTARIO

an Ontario government agency
un organisme du gouvernement de l'Ont

Canada

Guernica Editions Inc. acknowledges the support of the Canada Council for the Arts and the Ontario Arts Council. The Ontario Arts Council is an agency of the Government of Ontario.

We acknowledge the financial support of the Government of Canada.

elana wolff

everybody knows a ghost

GUERNICA EDITIONS

TORONTO – BUFFALO – LANCASTER (U.K.)

2026

Guernica founder: Antonio D'Alfonso

Michael Mirolla, editor
Cover and interior design: Errol F. Richardson

Guernica Editions Inc.
1241 Marble Rock Rd., Gananoque, (ON), Canada K7G 2V4
2250 Military Road, Tonawanda, N.Y. 14150-6000 U.S.A.
www.guernicaeditions.com

Distributors:
University of Toronto Press Distribution (UTP)
5201 Dufferin Street, Toronto (ON), Canada M3H 5T8
Independent Publishers Group (IPG)
814 N Franklin Street, Chicago, IL 60610, U.S.A.

First edition.
Printed in Canada.

Legal Deposit – First Quarter
Library of Congress Catalogue Card Number: 2025944737
Library and Archives Canada Cataloguing in Publication
Title: Everybody knows a ghost / Elana Wolff.
Names: Wolff, Elana, author.
Series: Essential poets ; 321.
Description: Series statement: Essential poets series ; 321
Identifiers: Canadiana 2025025980X | ISBN 9781778490224 (softcover)
Subjects: LCGFT: Poetry.
Classification: LCC PS8595.O5924 E935 2026 | DDC C811/.6—dc23

Poems

For M

"… shadows / wander in the dark, / their shapes the ghosts of day."
—from "Perigee Moon," by Sandra Barry

"What sort of world is this? Nothing is safe, and yet somehow even now I still feel everything will be okay."
—from *Like a Trophy from the Sun*, by Jason Heroux

"It is entirely conceivable that life's splendour forever lies in wait about each one of us in all its fullness but veiled from view, deep down, invisible, far off. It is there, though, not hostile, not reluctant, not deaf. If you summon it by the right word, but its right name, it will come."
—Franz Kafka, *Diaries*, October 18, 1921

Ghost. Altered. Probably after Flemish *gheest* < Middle English *goste* < Old English *gast* <akin to German *geist* < soul, spirit, demon < Indo-European *gheizd*, to be excited, to be frightened. Disembodied spirit < faint semblance < haunting memory < slight trace

Manu's sphere

may seem like a game of shades—

conjuring in the corridors, runes
on hidden lintels, demi-creatures

staging stunts, reminding us we dwell in many
nebulous worlds at once. Sirens

sounding human voices—
lower than infrared, higher than visible violet.

The city hoods its head
whenever the trouble comes,

it comes. The sea continues seeing, the rivers run, the
skies arise. The Queen

of the Night is back to life—her blóoms a resurrection,
Manu's eye-light preternaturally pale.

Bluish-white, he says, is a natural colour.
People may be right in saying it's strange,

we hold no hate. It flies
like a stick from our fingers, we draw and write.

Therein dwell the secrets—open as puzzles,
jugs and throats. The notion

that *agapē* is chaste
may be incorrect. Nevertheless, I love it.

And don't even think of speaking badly of Manu.

Kangaroo

January got you going—cut from mom,
her blue-light eyes and almond-

blossom smile. A third of her spirit entered with
Rafael—who tendered a piece of name for your sake.

We all want to swallow, be able to eat.
Eat you up means *Love you much.*

Tongue so near the lips, the gums, hope
sloping gastronomically

down our throats—like 'milk'
delivered in hanging

plastic bags by Kangaroo™ pump.
We've got supplies, a compact

crib, a matching mattress,
stroller with a pocket

for jejunostomy tubes.

Walking in the neighbourhood,
the park with the special

infant swing. Lying underneath the August
heat on the animal quilt. Your tiny clammy

arms & legs, long soft reaching feet.
The blue-light veins of your perfect head:

map to where we're going after this—

Concertina

Think of all the times you haven't been thwarted
by your teeth & tongue,

your clavicle & ulnas, femurs & gut.
Body says, *This one's on me.*

Brain says, *What's remembered lives,*
It's alright not to get over loss.

Light left Vega when you were born,
it's taken this long to arrive;

a run begun in a great bright kite
the ancients called a lyre.

(You are always the centre of the poem,
even when you're not.)

Just before imploding, a giant
star releases a tone (we're told)

that's close to middle C ~
Do stars relinquish sound?

If they do, can we hear it?
Beyond the poem are sirens, fire,

sea careening the pier. Beyond the poem,
a brother burned.

It's his exigency pushing the poem—
through to the flume

below. A hawk & swallow chorus rises—
higher than a hope. A truck

down-gears, a horn lets go. Sounds
that keep us piqued (you loathe the racket).

The whole wide world's a narrow bridge, a
concertina wire. The key is not to fear,

to make it across—

Sun Colours, Deep Field

There was lingering—a scent, a gentle
knelling sound a body could trust.
And lemony yellow, fennel green,
a whimpering over milk.
Sheer loveliness of rosy gummy gums.

Looking up is the essential vertical gesture,
I recently read: infants in the arms of mom,
their open, soulful gaze.
You don't command them, *Look at me*.
Instinctively and sweetly, they just do.

There's vehemence
to leaving a place
one didn't intend to leave so soon,
abruptly. If loving once meant tending,
it's now refrain. A deeper field of longing,
where earlier, it seems, mere wanting lay.

Use of the Room

We were rained
out of Algonquin Park, out of
our makeshift tent. L
ucky we found a motelier
willing to let us
ten-to-a-room; the grandparents
got the bed, the grandkids squeez
ed between them, feet-to-head.
The wall-clock, like a Cyclops

, stopped to watch: our dreams
tipped into twisty images; frozen star
es—yours and mine—like stags'
on mouldy shag; you and I
got the rug, the baby
stowed in the ark of a pulled-out
drawer. At random, like a biblio-

mant, I opened Gideon's
Bible to Isaiah 12:3—
With joy you will draw water
from the wells of salvation.
Our camp-stuff
hung like outsize tinsel,
wet on a room-shaped tree.

What I'm getting at is people
build up meaning between them
selves and all
the seemingly
random things
                that present.
What matters is contending with
these afresh.

Entering the painter's space,

you see the atmospherics, feel
the common centre where
the eye slides
back of the brush. Flat field,
blown grass, billowing
blue you'd take for sky is water:
                                        true or false?

Count on contradiction, un-
expectedness, a link:
St. Elmo's rain, anticipation—
soon, of seeing sun.

Sun will not be sun alone
and trees not only trees.

Lead me to the lean-to where you paint. There, a window
frames a Sitka spruce,
her drapey raiment;
a flimsy wishing-
nest of mourning doves—interpreter-angels—
scrying sky
we've all seen holding

heaven touching down, in lines
as slant
            as ladders,
piercing pink to cyan-
violet sea to beetle green.

Perpetually, the empathy of bent
& clinging colour.

Winter Work

The canvas where the easel stands extends beyond the art.
Tumid puce,
dark
curdled blue.
A dirty family shambles gessoed /

white—

on ache
that grew too furious,
I paint it to allay—against the dig of cynics;
name it for a phrase
in Kafka's winter work,
                    Das Schloss.
(One doesn't need a gloss.)

Snows have been alighting through the night.
Creatures—squirrels, rabbits, mice—
little figures,
subtle in the hush.

These animals,
their shadows—how it happens can't be tapped—
go white
to empathize,
          ceding me
the clemency of quiet.

          I am most moved
                    by figures that don't
whimper when they shift.

Lit Like This

I went there to be spared for a while. Nineteen, wasn't I?
I'd read *Poor Folk*, felt Russian—
kinship in a clause,
Not a sound to be heard from these people.
I—silent with fire to be elsewhere,
other than. How going away
can pare one back.
Not to belong
to any one set, only
not to be this. My best friends
were books. I squeezed the air from them, drew
my own sense of breathless.
Oh, I read many things, had a teacher who tutored me
in her off-hours, nudged me onto her son.
I bucked that sedulous kind of pressure
and fled.
Didn't know who to return to.

I come from a teetering type. Body
asymmetric—slant.
Knocking knees, a gammy hand,
drop-foot
and an eye set too far
into my skull, too big—
sometimes jaded,
sometimes yellow—a colour in curtains
& autumn leaves. A flicker-
tint uncommon in humans.

I've bit my lips and bled them
by a force I didn't know.
(Does anyone ever
know the inner goads?)

Yet leaning my head
against your chest—sometimes I relent:
My otherness
is undercut and quelled
          a little bit.

All night, a blur of light—now dull,
now shining
          up the shutters,

over the sheets & spread
          you call the anvil
for its weight. I have nothing

          to nudge you for; beam you
out of your horizontal
peace. Sleeper, you dream

and rarely remember,
I'm afraid of closing my eyes:
          the light-shapes

play their games
through the top of my head. I must have done
something dark to be lit like this.

In dreams you're never the husband.
Though you lie beside me nightly,
          you're the shape that fades away,

leaving my mind
too nigh.   Maybe I'm not the wife.
You exhale and ignite in me

          a being with a burning
tongue & wings. Eerie opalescent fire
wheeling at my head. I jolt awake

and still, you're here.
I mean, who am I
          to believe in dreams?

Adept

Grass rose deftly
every spring the strands
and damsels—ladies veiled and praying
souls that mingled with the music
from the upright in the den.
        Staves of slender
stems with little wings
leapt into my fingers.
I played them, never well, yet with esprit.
        Grandma was an adept.
She played the old pump organ at the schoolhouse
for the choir. God of middle earth
arose and quaked one day at practice.
The children fled, but Grandma kept on pumping, playing,
raising her excellent mezzo to the heavens.
Only when the vase of flowers
slid across the organ-top
and toppled
to her lap, did Grandma see
the floor beneath her
                shaking.
She grabbed her notes and fled as desks and chairs,
like rebels, slid across the schoolroom
into the floor. The organ—as she told the story—
fell with full
vibrato to the depths,
swallowed in a mouthful, just like Korach.
Grandma had a saying, *Praise the Lord*
but keep your wits.
                Not a living thing
was hurt in the quake.
The damaged floor was later
restored, the furniture replaced.
Grandma called it, *Miracle Revealed.*

The flowers and the vase
were soon recovered in the yard—
all-of-a-piece, upright,
unscathed.
        Even the water, she said, was
in the vase.

Garden Yellows

Begonia, you came back from brown—
I had the happy
hunch to plant you
southwest, by the door.

Potentilla—star-
face kisses
fallen to the garden arts.
They'll never call you kebab!

Daisy eyes, I see my wiles
reflected in your pithy discs. Whatever
the next shenanigan, I know
you know
        I'll fill it.

The plastic tab on the foxglove stalk—
a sale tag on a tall girl's
vintage dress. Time to cut it off.
(The tag, that is, not the frock.)

Fire hydrant, ever-shiny, mars the yard
yet guards the stealthy water-
nymphs that dwell
in ducts and culverts
under the lot.
            How it loves
that subternatural stuff.

The mulberry
leaf that's landed on
the flagstone by the lilac;
it's yellowed,
since the blue of green is out—

Behemoth of the Salt Lick

The sun shone dull as a bruise,
the wind soughed
slyly as an alibi—
civet-scented, kit & caboodle.
That's right.

Quite the animal
girl I was—tender of mice
and gerbils, hamsters, turtles,
fish, a talking bird, a tabby.

But love
took form
in a small, flop-eared albino—
                                        Cavia porcellus.
She squealed, she scratched,
she bit,
I held her,
fed her lettuce, roots
and vittles, changed her pine-chip bed. To me
she was *Behemoth of the salt lick.*
She understood the work: the fierce
commitment she instilled in me
to care with special fervour
for a peevish
pink-eyed pet.

            A milky scrim
spread over her eyes
one day she ceased to eat. I felt completely
stunted as she waned.
Someone, maybe my mother, suggested
we bring her to the vet.
Put down your little pig, he said,
and took her.

The sun shone angrily that day,
white-hot the next
and next. Then xanthous as a bruise
when it turns from purple.

Forty Years

have passed; we've left the desert.
Fire-pillar guides by night, cover of cloud-

like shepherds by day;
food & drink provided despite

our waywardness, especially mine.
I begged to linger; loved the camel-

coloured sand, the arid air.
Forty—that pivotal biblical figure;

we had to complete the course, I guess,
to leave—

Frigid winds are wringing here
I'm quavering in my coat—the slider on the zipper

stuck in the stop. You in your thermal socks
& flannels can't get warmth enough.

My laptop keeps demanding my location.
I must be a person

of deep belief. Every morning
I wake with the clock, to disembodied

radio voices, you beside me energizing. Sun
still pallid as ash. I'm certain it will quicken to its task.

What need have we of fear—

of slipping
on our winter

chinks of light.

Ice-lace

I went forward, biting wind. Cold
created ice-lace in my nostrils,

crinkled my skin. *Nobody needed to know*
where I come from. Snow

descended, blinding as a blast
and didn't ask. We landed

in the same dank class
at opposite ends of the table. My binder

broke, you fixed it
with a tool you brought to school.

Verily, I say, my heart enlarged.

Nothing have I kept by way of relic
from that passage, the building

with its mouldy rooms, was wrecked.
The room we sleep in now

has seven windows and a sleigh bed. Snow
continues falling—light as edelweiss

& starshine. Deftly and for everyone—
the beauty of the beam, of what is see-through.

As for disappearance,
it behaves the way of veils—gauzily

and thin as pre-existence.

Knocking the Next

We rise to shining life,
then turn—

lungs to earth,
liver to river,
kidneys to constellations;

heart of the recent
being knocking the next.

I am for the dark wood,
for the slick, invincible mountain.
I am for the noble gases, buck-
tooth moon and lithium salts,
[atropine, adrenaline, cardiac defibrillation]
empty meadow
fossils and their calm.
I lay my head
to enter sleep and murmur to a maker—
unknowable yet knowing.

You want a cat to have a tail
but some are born without;
expect four limbs on a human person,
some are only core:

I stand within
the timbre of a that one,
essentially trunk.
Thankful for my gravity
and ballast.

One Act with the Night Wolf

How did you hear of the moon, Lupu?
Think about it.

If you believe in mystery, step here.
Watch your footing.

When you go for night walks,
do you look where you're going, what's there,

or the sky?
Star shards. Hanging out.

Do you bring your woes along?
If so, from one to five—

five being the freest—would you let them
fall away?

The work of the Lord is in pieces.

Let's roll in the smoky
snow for a change.

It's a green light for wolves tonight,
moon the nearest I've ever seen.

Swing low for it, Lupu.
So pellucid pink, we could howl

to our favourite tunes.
Mine are named for trees in the street:

beech, oak, up from ash—
ascending to the spheres.

Unshielded as the satellite.
And could it care less.
This isn't a question, Lupu.

I'm not listening for answers.

Porthole to the Shades

One wall in the room on V— Street
sponges up the morning sun, mellows it,
and warms. This is the room I go to for repose,
it holds no dark—none, at least, that harms.

Years ago we rented in Jerusalem for the year—
a dusky ground-floor suite with a brambly garden.
A daughter had stabbed her boyfriend
in the kitchen there;

he succumbed.
I didn't learn of the killing
until after we'd signed the lease.
Of course we didn't tell the children.

The drain in the kitchen floor would sometimes make
a hollow gurgling sound. Every so often it belched
dark viscous liquid. The plumber fixed the belching
but a groaning tone set in.

Once I left the children home alone
to run some errands; returned to find them
side-by-side, immobile on the sofa,
faces pale, eyes gigantic globes.

Everything about the picture was wrong.
As though my stepping out had torn a porthole
to the shades. And errands at the pharmacy and bakery
and bank signalled my remissness.

You went and left us here alone,
                    the older one reproached.
There was screaming in the kitchen—loud—
        like someone being killed—

At the Heart of the Ghost

is death. Constructed from the mysteries
and morphologies of life. Persons,
their deteriorations, creatures
and their echoes. Hosts
of probability that death is not oblivion,
not emptiness, nor null. That life
has such perdurable charge, such synergetic forces
it continues unabated in the after-
Earth—albeit switched.
                                        Every now and then
a buzz, or glimpse, a wisp affirms this—
traces adumbrated of a verisimilar
inverse. For which one feels at times
a pull that's criminal.

Descant

If we have to supplement our days
with metaphysics,

let it be distinct enough to dazzle balance
and void.

Now that our life is half-
behind, there's no such thing as forwarding its forces.

No such thing as
backing into death, or after-
life: our word for the biggest wish.
Humour, if it enters there, must come with a *boo*

and a *ha*—that after sun has been revoked,
night is so Antarctic-sharp, it glints.

The night-soul chorus hums to us—the living still—
ineffably, as descant to our hope—

that what is sense-perceptible
transcends—

The Way She Worked

Barbara painted tiny rugs, embellished them with ink—
the kind that comes to life

with mythical thinking.
She might have chosen other means

than fine, exacting strokes,
but so loved Istanbul, the Grand Bazaar, the turquoise

palaces, the waters and the mosques,
the skies. And that's the way she worked.

Look, a decorated horse. The golden-
red chiaroscuro glows—

I'll ride him saddle seat
and he won't throw me. In private

re-enactment, I'm among the antique flyers.
From on high, I watch an entourage—

a line of inklings
wending down a hillside

                    to a strand. Everything these pilgrims own
is added to their backs. It's hard to understand their will to walk,

and yet it's not:
          A woman in a flowing robe and diadem is leading.

Rays are falling on the carpets waiting to be claimed.
Into art does not mean out of reach.

Spruce,

your fruit-like
decorations, trunk
a post of information:
          ring, hard,
          bark, hush.

I turn & touch
your husk & stroke
your pins & needles;
                              quiver—

I'm no more than your dark sap, Spruce,
a branch, no more than whorls,
the ghosting

          wind around your boughs
that bow. No more than the crusted
snow on your numbed
berm, falling
          flakes that form on specks of dust.

No-more-than-cones
in the human eye
          perceive more shades of green than any
other colour, Spruce: *Could you know?*

I touch my tongue to you & taste your texture,
pen & whet
these letters.
I'm word for you, Spruce,

needle for leaf,
cone for fruit,
templated,
redolent—
border-
blue through.

O-zone

A junco came to the window
                                        today I'm trying to think

like a bird. Bird-
brain gets a bad rap. That's bigism for you. Think little,

think syllable: If any can follow this, any
reality can. Breeze, breath, tread of a

bear in the yard.
It's easy to mistake

forbearance for fear,
bear for bird. Both

use claws like fingers
for a wide array of tasks;

and kiss, call, summon,
warn. May even grieve. Like us.

Hull fruit, skin fish, dig. Are militant—
if they need to be.

          Is that a hint of ozone in the hallway?
You thought the bear

was so far off,
we couldn't possibly

sense a tread, hear or see him
nearing. That smell is our leavened breath.

We're so focused on what we don't see,
we almost feel

                    feet in the garden, furry
forearms, flutter in the fir. Almost

sense a bear between us,
                                        a beak.

Low under indigo,

hull of the day.
Two across Formica sitting
underneath a metal ceiling
lit by pinpoint stars.
The land outside is incognito—
eddy in the rattle of a storm.
Trees along the track
are great galoots
in grubby habits,
grabbing at the glass
in mad abandon.
Before the wind
they'd stood aloof,
at attention,
dutiful—
simply watching trains
and passing wildlife.
Anyone can understand
they can't be wooden
totems always,
especially not in moody
mid-December.
I lean against the window,
feel their heaving
hitch my breath.
Your face
in dotted dark
is parsed—
a noun,
an apparition.

Noon

a slender slot on the clock. Across the street,
the concrete tower brandishes its power;
I am bogie—brake to bone.
Something from the building
drops. I don't know what
but suddenly I'm humming—
a gloomy tune and words that aren't my own:
Do not forsake me, oh my darlin'…
It seems almost heroic that the sky beyond the building
is a giant vibrant blue. A long, untroubled
tuneless blue—although it's noon, the time is nigh.
In the dream that brought me down,
the baby was located—
deathly still yet breathing in the dust beneath the couch.

Fishing with DB

Down we went with a one-two-three
to the riverbank
and sat. Hooks & lines, our poles,

a bucket of bait.
DB didn't have much to say, but his fingers
were pretty nimble & he hooked the worms

for us both. I felt his breath, the
nearness. Maybe it was the worms,
the muddy riverbank—something stank.

We sat there at the water's edge,
holding our poles between our knees,
waiting in the breeze

                    for a fish. Pert as punctuation.
I looked at him out of the side of my eye,
his forelock swung & caught the sun.

The hair on his arm was blond, on his shin
and thigh a powdery-white.
I saw my darker leg-hair then

and wanted madly to hide it,
crossed my legs and leaned on my knees,
which made it hard to hold the pole.

Dragonflies were skimming the river, shimmering
pink, a bluish-green. So beautiful, I wrote in a poem,
I forgot my leg-hair and DB's, the stink.

In that rendition, he and I felt a simultaneous tug.
We caught a fish together and the bone of our strangeness
broke. Returning to that version, I had to revise:

We didn't catch a fish together, and never met up again.
That moment of awakening to differences, and hair,
is hyped, like adolescence, to im/perfection.

Loquats

Blossom in autumn, fruit in spring. Linty little heads
with pearly pits—we would collect them.

For playing jacks and gems, and they were free.
A syrup from the flesh was said to cure colds,

a stuffy nose. The twigs were good for making figures—
mothers, fathers, stick kids.

I'm missing when I think of these, and hand-me-downs
and borrowed books. The foldout cardboard

keyboard meant for practicing at home—
for those who didn't have a real piano. Until

we got an upright of our own. I only got to hear
the sound my fingers made at school—

before the other children in the class.
I'm missing when I think of this and the kiss

I didn't get from one I loved (or thought I did), then
the kiss I got from one I didn't. A sadness over this

migrated, limb-like under my ribs—paining
when I breathed, especially deeply.

I'm present when I think of what one does to palliate:
break the syntax, snap it at the trunk, the inner rings.

Spring will reach the window like an angry
daughter and son. You can't ignore what they've done,

you've done.
How do you howl if you don't express it; sing

and not cry out—freely and profusely—like the loquats
blooming in fall.

Gloss

Blue at the back of the trees—
the tarp that never has to be fastened,

air on air.
The chariot that crossed the sky on wheels in wheels—

a fugitive
to every revolution.

Every new one
knows the mother's voice from in the dark, mother-

pulse within the womb
& father in the /y/. Parrots—their electric cries

& siblings in the s/wings.
Jackals crying through the night

like corybantic cousins. The city
I take to bed, like kith,

on my skin. The flinty, sticky city,
its quotidian things & mysteries.

Blues beyond the pines and pine-
cones silent overhead,

like thought—the kind of thought
that's prayer, for thought is prayer enough,

unuttered. If you lose the words,
just think in pictures. If you need a tune,

just pick one up.

Sleight

Dawn, the quick of day, its rinse
of indigo before the din—

the drubbing city hoo-ha.
Dawn the nimblest hour,

how it rises up and dials.

Yesterday, black storks
came sailing—high in the thermal air above Arbel—

circling like a crown of kingly skippers,
listing in a language

matching silence.

They looked so lightly brushed
& unencumbered.

Then the flirt & draw of glint & glitter in the offing—
a reservoir? a tarn?

We walked along the path, the glitter

bid—by sleight of land
or eye. Blue immovable sky, the watery

body constantly shifting. Like longing,
like a numbness, and its drubbing …

What rupture have I let into my flesh?

After-cast

Those who grew up
under trouble learned to do with less: no second helpings;
hand-me-downs—whatever the cut or colour.
Waste not, waste not, want—

The yard was frugal too.
Witchgrass, plants that toughed their way
each spring from stubborn soil. Snowdrops, yarrow,
Lenten rose. Nana was a saver.

She swaddled a book in gauzy cloth,
kept it like a miser
keeps his wealth,
and never wept. Or if she did,

it would have been into her pillow-slip, in secret.
The image that returns to me is pressed—
a butterfly, her serving tray (she never used for serving)—
real dead bodies

flattened under glass. Wings
so luminous blue
they shimmered orange under my lids:
the after-cast of gazing at them, dreamily,

then closing my eyes.
Everybody knows a ghost, said Nana
on the sand one day.
We were sitting side-by-side, gazing at the bay.

I had a child's idea of ghost—a gauzy,
pillow-slip figure. Also the hidden thing
in plants that Nana called perennials—because they die
and come to life each spring. Butterfly-

blue transformed to orange
wings on my inner lids—my shimmery
notion of ghost. Nana, I suppose,
though, meant some tough, intractable
pith.

Gmünd, 1920 / 2019

In a border town by a dingy inn
that looked to be

designed by rogue committee, I saw
two figures gliding by, like proof,

but not in flesh;
I nudged you, Look, it's them—

Milena Jesenská and Franz!
There, on the other side of the street,

walking past that billboard—
severed from us by nothing but dust

and air, the drape of the veil—
the one that buffers

simultaneous time and sometimes
drops.

They must be here for us,
I said, *to share the burden of hurt*

they felt that hazy day they met here,
humbled by their hollow hopes …

I can relate to those.

You nodded, absent-mindedly, then pointed—
Look, that sign—Tom Jones *LIVE*

next month right here in Gmünd!
Who would've thought Tom Jones would play

a border burg like this, you snickered.
I was looking past the sign—the billboard,

down the street. The pale retreating
couple on the other side of dust.

Throwback

Wind wrinkled the river and lake,
the clouds—
huge cumulo-vaporous shapes—
flattened into stratus: long thin aerial altars

disassembling in the mist.
In school we called an awkward boy 'The Emu'
behind his back. Legs too long for his body,
head too small, he walked like a logger. He went completely

bald before grade twelve and moved away. Odd
how people pop into one's thoughts.
Mr. P. was my German teacher that year.
A fit man with a moustache that looked like Hitler's—

which only occurred to me later; at the time,
I liked his tidy style. His potent way of pacing—
back and forth across the room. His turtlenecks
and dark blue suits, how he called on Anne von Glatz

and Elsa Metz to answer. He made me like those
clipped Germanic names and love those girls,
even though they hardly noticed me. Mr. P.—
I might have called him late one night,

for help. But I didn't have his number
or know what I'd tell him if I'd had it.
Sometimes he would sit on his desk
and show the soles of his brogues. Mystery

emanated from the leather.
I copied his strong, deliberate script—letters slanting right
like duteous feet.
She who copies becomes the stalker, I read

and abandoned that slant.
He showed up some months later
where I was waiting on cocktail tables, ordered a Scotch
and water and asked me what I was doing these days—

as if he couldn't see. I'm working to pay my way,
I said, and smiled and went on serving.
Seeing him there—that moustache
and the turtleneck, the dark blue suit—

was weirdly out of place.
I felt his tidy eyes on me
wherever I was in the room.
Je vous en prie, I answered, when he thanked me

for my service.
He took my hand and pressed
a lavish tip into my palm, closed his fingers over mine
and wished me, Alles gute.

Perhaps
it was from Mr. P.
I first heard tell of Kafka.

Aries in the vernal vault,

spring in its beginnings.
Throb at the back of the forest, auguring,

Egg
of the immanent imminent— Earth

in her glyphic posture: on all fours—⊕—
bequeathing

green. The water
under the ice on the pond

humming its tonic song.

My heart
ajar: large as a milk leg.

*

There are places on the forest
floor where light arrives

like beads of sweat: from the dermis—up.

The earth a weighty
darkness, an immense and loaming

dark from which a vital light
arises. The light may be invisible

and yet one feels the lightness
and the green, the shining

darkness of the larging
heart ajar—

Tapioca

Mom made tapioca pudding—fluffed up
airy light with egg whites, sugar, real vanilla.
The pearly tapiocas felt like eyeballs in my mouth—

tiny eyeballs swilled in milk. Swallowing felt sweet,
and slightly sinful. The more I swallowed,
the better I felt, the more I wanted

that tingle. Once I downed an entire bowl
before it had time to set.
Mom rarely made the pudding after that

there were bigger changes. I miss that tapioca,
have never been able to reproduce its globular froth and
flavour, its blend of transgressive and good.

My fella likes his mother's dishes—the way
she always made them. Mine are adaptations—
vegetarian goulash, paprikash. Nothing with onion

or garlic. 'Paradise' and 'tomato' share a word
in my fella's mother tongue: *paradiscom*.
He loves tomatoes—beefsteak, cherry, heirloom,

hothouse, plum. All except the green ones,
which summon up a tea he was given in childhood
to stop the runs. My fella likes to eat his dinner

in peace. His hours at the office are long;
mine are adjusted to fit.
I look at myself, see codes that won't be cracked.

Luckily, my fella is discreet. He knows to leave
some things unasked, unsaid.
Ellipsis is a fine device—in writing, also in life.

Our bed in the place on V— Street faces east.
The other morning my fella shouted—loud
from the living room, *A giant roach*

is crossing into the kitchen.
I heard him whack it, flush it down.
It's the humidity, he said. We'll have to keep the windows

shut, at least while the nights
are hot. By the way, did you know?
Cockroach blood is milky-white.

One hardly sees the stars these nights—
manmade lighting dominates the skyline.
We sometimes fall asleep to the light of our screens,

but mostly not. These are lights we control
when we choose to—
lie in semi-darkness of the ever-electrified city.

After a while, we give in to the night,
to where we're carried, who knows where, for what—
we give up most of our consciousness in slumber.

And when I wake beside you, the moments at the threshold
evanesce: I love this word, its whisper
and hiss, the tingle it elicits—

Touch-No-Matter-What

We may have taken the higher road,
we may have taken the low.
Crossed alluvial fans and buttes,
steppes,
plateaus,
a rift zone. The weather we remember
always death-
defying sun. Unifying,
touch-no-matter-what-the-distance sun.
Things were happening at the borders,
at so many borders,
after years of living
folks had come to call
                    the places home.
Shapes have been erupting
that contain an inborn form. Stars
the hearts of hoya flowers,
pink becoming rose. Tones
the mandevillas bring
on opening their throats: salmon, madder,
garnet, ruby, scarlet—

only darker.
The darknesses are different here and light
          of indecipherable design.

Our suitcases
that went astray on crossing, on the way,
arrived the other day and in them
things we didn't pack.

Gods of August

The black that comes from scratching
my scalp
collects
beneath my nails. What soot is this? What ash?

A new wound
opens in my foot
and mushrooms
like a gillyflower star-

patch to my thigh. Beautiful hurt—
I spread it
with a salve
and it is dressed.

The doves that come to nest
inside the window-bars
are pests. They coo
and poop and kill the plants. I water-

gun them off—these noisy,
messy emblems of peace.

I'm up and down
like arrows, flies,
a fiddler's arm, a windsock.
These days the wind—

so hot and fraught—projects
its vaunting voice like gods of August.

We spoke last night across the ocean—
on the call
you heard the howl, as if, despite the miles, its heat
was nearer than your ear.

Luna

You are full of glitches and I write my little songs.

You grin like a backhand slap; I sit and scribble.
One in stone and one / aloneness; bed or breakfast,

which came first … arm or charm or harm …

The secrecies of outer / inner. Flips & language bits
& seeing these as p/art of poetry's work.

And choosing from among the waiting words

to make them fit—in lines that might be said
to right themselves. I cast a piece with you herein,

your takes and your mistakes. You gave your face

for free, like Carrie Fisher signed her girlhood likeness—
Princess Leia—over to Lucas. I claim your beauty too:

radiant in phases, grand and warm; at other times, ethereal,

oblique. I'll see you at the waterfall tonight.
The song of falling water blankets the sadness. Yes,

I'll be alone. You will be alone as well.

Corroborate the Audio

A distant ring
right here
behind my head, a
thin falsetto—

as if I'm some place
high
in middle Europe—

die böhmische Seite des Berges

The lighting
suddenly problematic. Umbras
swatting walls like time
dividing

or collapsing,
and no one to corroborate
the audio.

The lighting dims,
the shadows
fold. I lie
in distant dark—

die böhmische Seite des Berges
disappears from the ring
of as if,
and silence is relieved,
like time,
of the burden

of being heard.

Refinement

Once there was a brakeman who was so musical
he became a conductor. One day, transported
by the majesty of the music, he dropped his baton
mid-movement.
                The stick signalled from the stage,
Shouldn't you pick me up?
                                        I don't really need you
after all, the conductor quipped, dismissing the tool,
and pleased himself with waving his hands orchestrally
in the air, the tails of his jacket flapping at the audience.

Screwdriver

Do ideas simply rise, like surfacing from slumber—
seeing the ceiling, feeling the sheets;

you here breathing morning into the window
side of the bed, tailing, maybe,

the end of a dream
of things that fly in the night—

I'm wearing
a long black cloak & boots, piloting a broom-

stick. You've brought your cosmic tool-
kit—prepped for a starlit trip.

It could be my projection, but I sense
you're getting ready to fix: a clicker? a widget?

My zipper?

You've got your Robertson #1—the one
they found and confiscated,

bits & all, at bag check. Yet here it is,
the thing in itself

as real as the steel of its shank—
high-grade & Canadian-made; transcendent—

Catalytic

When I weary of being woman,

I think of the golden cherubs
on the lid of the holy ark,

their ever-touching wings

above their faces & the space between.
How in a single instance

fire issued swiftly from that space—

arrowed along the tent of meeting,
entered the priestly nostrils of Aaron's

sons, Nadav and Avihu,

& burned their souls
for offering alien incense.

I try to imagine the angle

of that fire—as it issued.
How it streamed,

then struck. I focus on the cherubs' wing-

tips, where they join—
        they're made that way.

When I weary of being woman,

I think of that gripping centre-point,
the catalytic effect of being thus-

charged, & unremitting.

Beam Me Up

After winning a prize, says Souv,
the pressure to be nice,
    not tired,
is high.
And titles start haunting the text.

Like all the loves who ever left—ghosts as old as Ur
Kasdim
put their stock in metem-
psychosis and got it.

I wish I were a better spectre. Damage
undermines me every time.
The bruising at the neck has passed,
the rest of me is next.

Maybe I'll fly;
    I've got the sheets.
Or maybe I'll make an angel in snow,
                    blend in.
(Once I would have thought that meant
        I was giving in to influence.)

Moonlight's
sliced to lines tonight
by tines of the neighbour's gate.
        What if I have one beam me up?

I'm low on breath, so tired,
            and they're playing the exit tune.

Holy Mo—
"A Little Night Music,"
            again—

Why Verify That Rain

I travelled in re-
verse and viewed a reel:
our younger selves,
the two of us, the tour group
at Buchenwald,
assembled in the yard beyond the ovens

listening to the guide describe,
in Deutsch-
inflected English,
                    what was done.
The sky grew grey,
a thin
rain fell
on only you and me—
a chute
from cloud
to ground.

It wet our coats, our shaken faces,
stopped,
and we continued.
The others in the group were dry.
Sky, a living witness.

We're in another century now.
Why slither
down the stalky
stretch of memory. Why want
to verify that rain—
whether it fell,
if only on us.

Why not simply trust?

The way I trusted my mother
saying I walked
the day I crawled—
because of the sisal roughness
of the rug on my infant knees.
The way you trusted your mother
when she came to you—
transparent—
in the keenness of a dream,
and said, though not in living words,
I'm all right where I am
and I can see.

Dear Frankie on Falster,

Thank you for the postcard. The picture has a kind of
Wes Anderson set-deliberateness to it. Quirky, natural
yet surreal. I can almost see you sitting inside that booth—
together with the ghost of Monsieur Hulot—*en vacances.*
Both of you looking out on the waters, smiling at the horizon.
The main point being that there is no point, only 'main'—
in the archaic meaning of 'open ocean'.

It's wonderful that you need not think of heating,
but what are you doing for a hat?! I'm wearing the boater
you left on the rack. Getting inside your head. Sky above us—
overseeing no mean deed, nothing ugly. Just the stillness
of lizards. I wish that for you, and happy returns!

I've got pink delphiniums in the vase. According
to the old-time saying, they stand for youth and renewal.
I'm including them here—for renewal is always nearer
than we think, even if youth is not. The pole atop
the booth is a lot like you—tall, thin, singular.
And the tracks on the sand bring to mind traces
of sea creatures—jelly faces you may have stepped on
in your walks along the strand. Your innocent footprints,
and summer just begun.

Hugs,

Your e

Kangaroony

We're eating pizza on D— Street.
(I've never noticed the name of the place). Purim

now behind us, Manu wearing his elf ears
still; they don't even look ironic. He's at the age

of feeling unselfconscious
strength in a getup. We're at a time of rising

world unrest.
The twins are wearing pizza cheese, the smaller one

bespattered with goopy red sauce. He's come through
half his life (so far) hooked to plastic tubes. Slap-

happy to be eating on his own, and making a mess.
A dad with a cat tattoo on his cheek

is just as jaunty as us, joking with his kids
two tables away. We'll go for ice cream after this—

pink bubblegum flavour
with sprinkles & chocolate chips. All the yummy stuff

that fits in a cup. We'll do the Kangaroony
on the way from here to there,

holding hands & one-two-three—*jump up!*
The little twin so light his legs lift off like wagtail wings—

He's unaware (for now) of worldly strife.
And blessed, as you've said, to be given the gift of life.

Infinity-love

My short translation of Kafka sails away
above a lake, rigged as a cloud-shaped barque.
An up-gust meets the movement and torpidity
of the text—a piece that chugs, unbudging,
through its syntax. Not to be stopped by wor(l)ds.
Waters breaking in and out, boundaries dis-
integrating, white bears losing their ice.
The breezes stream rhapsodic—
summer in winter in spring in summer in fall.
The sails of the barque-shaped cloud
as high and light as infinity-love, which fills us
with its cotton batting, warms us like enthusiasm—
godly.
In the village of my synonyms, barque is a brilliant mist.

Docent

Stillman Secondhand Books closed up for good the week
before I arrived—looking to buy a novel to read to my mother
during my visit. I thought of Anita Brookner: *Undue Influence,*
Providence, Leaving Home, or Strangers. Something subtle,

elegiac, yet clarion. As I stood before the store—now grey
vacated space—a thin-winged docent: Monarch
butterfly brushed my cheek & fluttered up.
I felt bewildered, mystified—couldn't say exactly what …

Okay: de-
boned, shucked, un-
guided too, yet somehow beckoned …
You never can tell if an odd surprise will make it

over into a poem. Like you can't predict what you'll do
if someone deep in your life says suddenly *Go away.*
It may be their way of saying *Stay.*
A switch can be elliptic
& as deft as brush & flutter.

Restless

We stand aside & gaze across
the yard, the garden, shade

between the berms & weight of air.

The outer lights are dark,
the inner string completely lit: How's that?

Something like a hum, a buzz—

a rabbit in a smoky coat
lopes over, jolts, pricks up its ears.

This smile of yours—coquettish—says,

It must be faulty contact.
Or else some kind of sly

low-voltage pitch.

You can't rebut a hum, a buzz,
the evening breeze along the trees,

the brush of something sudden

from behind … a nubby work-shirt?
That flutter-

body feeling, too, tip-

toeing in the gloaming—so restless,
undomestic.

(One thinks of *Schadenfreude* tales
in which a casual rashness undoes lives.)

Or Else

These, your inner lamps, are lit in
          sultry summer breeze. Salty
heat, the nipping singe of the Sea—
                    so saline the moon itself
looks longing for water.

          A gun dog strains to reach behind
each passerby on the beach—

It must be part of the sentient soul
to hold this much desire.

You've grown into a milder
likeness, quieter,
finer drive.
Your lamps are lit in breathing breeze, in feeling
briny night heat;
          watching a Grey Ghost
                    frisk at the end of her tether;

humming a theme from a TV series
      streaming from the cellphone of a jogger …

slowing to hold my hand a little longer on the walk …

or else it's me
who's slowed,
and you are loyal.

Stuff That Stirs

A fuggy light, a balmy day,
Bob, our dog,
still horizontal

in bed.
I step outside, sit back to read a recent
book by Modiano

who writes of disappearance, loss,
oddly-named acquaintances
and long-gone loves

and canines; someone
always being sought, self and others
found, or not; doppelgängers,

fronts & bluffs—
stuff that stirs me up.

Sitting back, re/reading, I ascend into a reverie,
slip inside the blue-black
scrim of ink.

Hey there, says an inner voice,
Where would you put the soul,
sixth sense, this metaphysical static,

which makes it hard to hear
the reedy music.
Is it a harmonica? Are we on a mountain train?

I jolt awake, the book is lying sidewise
on my knee, a dog-eared *LOST DOG*
notice stuck in the gutter. *HE ANSWERS TO SHANGRI-LA—*

the notice says, I eye the silly name,
and our dog Bob comes bounding, like a telephonic foundling,
        into my lap.

On Listening to Philip Glass, *Violin Concerto No. 1*

I lie on the floor all afternoon,
playing Gidon Kremer
playing Glass. Broken chords, arpeggiated,
wafty stratospherics
falling—
at my belly, under wing, a churning inner timbre—air

as close to current, blood
& pulsing
          in & out

—the soloist & orchestra in ticking oscillation:
strict, propulsive
                    thrill—

Those drawings by a boy in middle
school who didn't speak, but drew—obsessively & deftly—
airplanes breaking up mid-air.

His pen & ink would move so quick—we gathered
round in awe to watch
                              Kazuo Watanabe
do his thing / repeat / repeat /

jumbos cracking up—his one motif.
Flung across the pages—bolts & rivets, like notation.
Fuselages, stabilizers,

slats & flaps & engines; gears—
                                        reams of silent pictures.
He left before the end of term,

we never exchanged a word.
I didn't think
to ask him for a sheet.

When It Comes

I hope to have the skill
for building sentences—politic, poetic

and alert. Not settle for a jingle-line like
Smash the Patriarchy. Not like he

whose tongue got tied
whenever he opened his mouth.

When it comes, I hope I won't be
shy to face the unrelated;

jettison my leery side;
be cabalistic as nine.

How any number multiplied by nine
reduces to nine: 9 × 3 is 27; 2 + 7 is 9.

How adding nine to any number
doesn't alter its digital foot. Take for instance

74885: 7 + 4 + 8 + 8 + 5 is 32, and 3 + 2 is 5.
9 + 7 + 4 + 8 + 8 + 5 reduces, likewise, to 5.

True-to-type in any combination every time.
Try it.

And if it doesn't come, then wait.
In waiting

hope to crack the coming skill-
set to abide it.

Cherry Compote

You're standing on the ladder
at the cherry tree and reaching—into the dark
serrated leaves, sliding

the ripened clusters into the bowl
you've brought to the ladder-top.
I'm predictably dizzy

down below, predictably stiff:
my movement stilled to thinking of what if …
a block falls, somebody's crushed—

the neighbourhood, the city,
everything in it …
My left hand on the ladder, right on you—as if

I'm holding you up.
I've sometimes thought of you happier elsewhere,
what if we'd never met?

Take the bowl. It's full, you say,
and hand it down to me. Whatever's left in the tree
is for the creatures.

I strip the stems and leaves and place the cherries
in a pot, add water. Boil, simmer,
mash. The pearly pits, released from their skins,

sit like shrunken skulls in crimson flesh.
I strain them out, *but what if*
one remains to crack a tooth—whose would it be …

A silly thing to think and then for some reflexive reason
I think of Pearl who told me out of the blue—
one day while we were chatting—that she sometimes breaks

into frantic
laughter she can't control

till she chokes.

Craning for That Port

Under sun's almighty eye
everything is wilting. We
sit in the yard
on the stand of stones—stiff
and contradictory.   Only corpses
give up contradiction

(and maybe not). We're struggling to hold
spirit and form—
          that fractious match—
together. Leave the pain
of old remissness out.
(It-sticks-like-a-tongue-to-a-metal-fence-in-winter.)

I've never felt like Duchess Someone,
nor like Olga or Anne
                    with another name.
But irrepressible, yes—
and craning for that port to preservation.
You—the royal you—likewise.

Hot, hot Sunday
evening, you and I on the circular
stand of stones; rise,
then get down
on our knees, dig in the yearning
earth and sow our seeds; feed them

Miracle Gro-Mix soil
and water from the well.

The spirits are breathing—
hear them, I say.
No, you counter. It's only
the heat raising vapour.

Spectral

It's possible to believe in a calm
anonymous kind of life. A
modest home in an older,
well-kept quarter of the city. A
couch for lounging and reading on,
watching what transpires
out the window. A lamp, its circle
of private light,
casting its eye on your pages. Laundry
on the fauteuil,
          dresses hanging to dry.

Outside, daily droppings on the pansies
in the window boxes: pigeons
roosting in the eaves and soffits
delivering dirt. There's hardly any way
to put an end to it.
          The folks across the alley
have a spunky Weimaraner. The daughter
takes him out three times a day. You'd exchange
hellos, if you crossed each other's path.

Out of view and earshot are the marchers
in their thousands. They've occupied
the streets and squares for years. Citizens
who have a stake in their lives here.

It's possible to believe in a quiet
spectral kind of life.

                    No one really sees you
coming and going,
               and where you're not

What Now

In the darkest month, I walked the dog offroad
and down the ravine.
                    Masked like sinister Santas,
a pack of coyotes
sprung from the brush—
moving their muzzles in unison, mewling
the seasonal tunes.
                              I hadn't counted on this.
Nor on the placards tacked to the trees, the dis-
embodied jingles.
Mystified by the presentation,
the dog re-
coiled and whimpered,
                                        I drew my Ruger LCP.
The pack deduced the rules,
removed the masks, but stood their ground.

               What now of the gun?
The "promise" to the audience—
that once it's drawn and cocked,
it's gotta go off.

Crow

I'm answered by a flyby—
past my windshield as I'm driving. Big and black
and winging like a crow—it is,
it must be
          you who answered when I asked which word
is better for the final line
of a poem I've been composing these many months:
adept or deft? Back and forth
I've been between the two—alike but not the same.
Crow, you know/you knew/you flew
before my wind-
shield suddenly & at the very second
I said *deft*—
          You've come to me in sundry ways
in country after country, over time I've come to see you
as a sure conversion figure. I ask, and in your manner, Crow,
you signal; I receive, believe.

*

          I fear they'll find your beak beneath my skin
one day compel me to confess that I'm a composite
gone wrong.
     To them I bear a scent of soap that's made with trace
of henbane leaves & tincture of white poppy seeds
that's said with regular use to raise the spirits,
to simulate flight.

Light from Water Where We Bothered It

Unlike books,
sky can't be remaindered—big as it is.
Tundra goes on, too, for miles and miles; I side with miles,
not klicks.
Overseas,
P.M.'s still writing vanishment
in every book; he does it better than well.
Like Cézanne painted apples, Monet
lilies, Turner seas.
Like Thomson painted northern trees,
Hockney
California pools,
Barnett Newman *The Stations of the Cross.*

My hair is whiting—badger stripes—
I cover them with pink.
Skin dimpling,
arches fallen,
knees & femurs
groaning bone.
What gives?

Light from water where we bothered it,

thermostats exactly where we set them.

Openness, refining-
work that's filigreed
to fit: the big steal,
quick switch, ever-

aching wait—

Three-prong Plugs Have Grounding Pins

Something above the window swings
an aleatory
shadow before
the towers across the street—they
                    block the daylight.
Vitreous floaters
double-
down
& the ficus trees—their eye-
shaped leaves are weeping.
If I listen hard to my feet, I hear the sinews
wailing too:

          What is going on
          inside this body?

                    My lower
lip has started to twitch I think
it must need water. I sit
to drink & drink the twitching
thankfully lets up.
The socket in the wall, I see: a perfectly
circular face,
two identical
spherical eyes, a mouth that's moulded
into an O of wow or dread—
not dread—it has to be wow—

          No nose
though it's implicit. Pareidolia fills it in. The wall,
as wide as women's wings. They're beautiful,
so beautiful, that if I try
to write them down—to pin them into simile,
I'll have missed.

Maybe I can swing one
into aleatory
shadow—
that's a thing—

In Winnipeg on the Centenary of Kafka's Death

The corner lot
I come to, all along it
grassy mounds.
Peek-a-boos from burrow holes—
a head appears,
a staring face,
another and another.
Here and there, alert,
up/down—
a colony of prairie dogs,
the fetishes:

domes and rims and entrances and

scampering and ramming hard

and chewing grass as sharp as perianal
scent and blades.

The detail of the tail.

Not like dogs' at all, these barks.
More like dolphins
throwing their voices

at crows. Kafka and my prairie-boy father
meet in the eye of my moiling mind
like sibs in transmigration

on this lot.
I watch a rodent show its nose. Hard to say
if it's out of the ground,
or in it.

These Snippets, Lustrous & Doubled

Man in a dress-
shirt under the tent—attentive
& with questions:
          What (from me) can he really want …

          I turn
& cough to my sleeve—
a past re-
peats (somewhat) like leaves … & surely

as a pen is held
above the page, awaiting,

we sh**a**re in our names a middle ‘**a**’—
like m**a**n—this m**a**n,
jackr**a**bbits
& l**a**w.
          Freedom,
fundamentally, is what
the law’s about, he says

the audience beneath the tent is listening
of their own accord.
We owe this
to the poems being
read,   a will to connect.

This box of Siamese
cherries I bought for lunch at Market Square.
Every one of them lustrous & doubled:

two-conjoined-in-one-
          continuous shiny
          crimson skin.

Canterbury Bells

Never mind they hang their heads
from spring

until December. Time
would pleat if it had tucked-buds

and purple petals like these—
whose scent is ever-slightly minty,

ring almost inaudible to humans. This woman
bends to listen, sniffs the mint

and steals a stem.
A chipmunk darts across the yard, pauses

at the gothic wall to watch.
Not to be caught in the act, the woman swivels

quick, & trips.
Never mind she tears her purple skirt

& skins her shins.
Campánula, in the language of flowers,

means thanks.

Juney, It's You

Greening like a lustre colour. Red and blue
birds flying to the heavens
all done up. The cumulus so nimble it collects to cauliflower-

cotton-masses just like batting—*presto*
as I write a tiny spider walks my wrist. In someone's culture
spiders crossing bodies must mean luck. Rain, a sudden

windfall, the cherry tree is fruiting. Hard green baubles
still the squirrels, vying with the starlings, come to feast.
Juney, it has to be you—I couldn't do this.

Or ring like Canterbury bells, or smell as deeply
sweet as spring syringa, or hang my head like Lily
of the valley crooning the garden nymphs, the dulcet parasol

mushrooms. Again, I've planted digitalis—hopefully she takes.
The light is low beneath the trees. The ants come marching
nonetheless—onward to the colony—led along by the pheromone

trail—over the subterranean stream. Sometimes we can feel its
flow—a silent reminder that most of what we feel cannot be seen.
Teeming in the etheric—all this given project.

Peony, my everlasting pink, you're so short-lived.

Sea Level

Now for the first time we see the grey waves of the North Sea
slapping the distance beyond the ship, the sound, if you will,
of slate. God in the fog and listing, the misting mime-

white horizon and sheep. Rubbing their wool-thick
shoulders with others on the slopes at Nordfjord.
Touch one, says the man, and be switched.

There's nothing wretched in being anonymous,
nothing disgraceful in being, as speedwell,
just one of a low-rising other. The long straight light-

lines curve, the waves send no lone gull up,
no puffin. The vista's complicit, ice-
water a primer—a leveller, says the man. The lower I am,

the truer my place. We gather on the upper deck at midnight,
tip our faces skyward—waiting to be amazed
by solar wind & swirling shimmer.

Bright Blue Stars

Lovely being seen in the tint of mist

behind a waterfall—listening
for the glistening

and a blink. Points of bright

blue stars—the indications—
how they signal.

If you die in the dream,

wake up. It must be fear of infinite
regress, the big abyss.

(Or phantom energy, negative mass, the Bang, the
Crunch, the Rip.) Remember—

hope

is
vertical,

and rises in resistance. Faith

requires yearning (and a leap).
Down here, it's a holding zone. Up there—

turtles all the way—

Make of it your revelatory
          work.

Phantom

It's gone now—my distinctive spot (called beauty)
below my lower lip. Removed
by the aesthetician with her radio frequency tool.

She said I wouldn't feel it at all, but pain
(as much as beauty) is a very subjective thing.

After the freezing and zapping off,
she burned the emptied area,
she said, to prevent a return.

The whole procedure took about an hour, give or take.
When I rose from the treatment table,

she showed me the piece of excised skin—
round and brown and ectoplasmic,
sitting on a swath of gauze.

She asked me if I'd like to take it home.
(What? I thought, and keep it?)

No, thanks, I said, I'll leave it with you,
and promptly left the room—a Band-Aid
over the treated spot, my step a good bit quicker.

I don't know what the future will bring—who does?
But I've come to this—

I've let a piece of my countenance
go, though it feels still like a phantom feature
planted plainly in my face.

Don't We Look Marvellous

The body becomes the vehicle

for the invisible

(faith in change?) I'm driving north on Bayview in a
whiteout,

it's been days—
                    I see you as I saw you in the hours

hooked to machines. Swollen,
cut & intubated,
sleeping.

Be strong, you said
before the prep, before they took you in,

before the wait—
          Isn't it strange?
An hour turns to another and another and the cryptic ticks …

The psalm that I repeated while you were under—

oozing and under:
Frail beings … grasses … sprouts of the field …

(It's not how you feel, it's how you look that counts,
said somebody else. Someone in your repertoire of quips.)

Don't leave till we leave together, I mouth
aloud to the cold car-air—driving home
          alone through snow.

This selfish self, this less-than-this
clutching the wheel—

Impromptu with an Emptying Pen

Let's celebrate the short days, hours,
glint of hard sharp snow.
Tired bones and jokes, the bed that isn't
big and firm enough,
the sheets that aren't so fresh.
Let's brook the fear of disappearing, bear
with those who won't bear back—
          this: the test,
the lesson.
Let's navigate by plain first lines
that link to closing words
like knell and nugget;
touch the windows filled with night,
tap dark's deep and radiating hearth.

Let's celebrate the short days, hours,
tap dark's deep and radiating hearth.

Larkspurs

—with a nod to Mark Strand (1934-2014)

In a yard the size of a sheet—
tomatoes, cabbage,
cucumbers grew. Vegetables for jarring
to eat in winter.
Flowers other than hollyhocks
and larkspur would have wasted space.
The 'Blacknights'
clung to the western wall.
The 'Galahads'
rose above the fence and seemed almost to float—
ice-white flowers clothed like ghosts.

Breath pulled into my chest
like thoughts to a coffin. Coffin
the body, the body a thought—give it up.

I give up my eyes, my ripe green pears.
I give up my nose, the moat of my throat.
I give up my ears, their cockles and muscles, my neck
that swans my chest.
I give up my arms above the wrist—
to liberate my fingers. My uterus
I gave up long ago, its inflammations;
tubes and trumpets, ovaries, the other
lower neck.
I give up both my breasts (Would I give just one?),
the cage beneath them. I give the light of my thighs,
my headstrong feet that contravene me.

The yard the size of a sheet
I give to the larkspurs wearing my white
petal dress. They wear it better
than I ever did. I was always
mostly out of my body.

Notes

Ghost: Definition adapted from the entry in *New Webster's Collegiate Dictionary*, 3rd edition. Victoria Neufelt, editor-in-chief. MacMillian, 1988.

Concertina: The lines "The whole wide world's a narrow bridge" and "The key is not to fear" are translated from the Hebrew song "Kol Ha-Olam Kulo"—lyrics attributed to Rabbi Nachman of Breslav, melody to Rabbi Baruch Chait. Jewish Women's Archive: https://jwa.org/media/lyrics-to-kol-haolam-kulo.

Winter Work: The phrase "dirty family shambles" ("schmutzigen Familienwirtschaft") is drawn from chapter 11 (In the Schoolhouse) of Franz Kafka's novel *Das Schloss / The Castle*. Translation by Mark Harman, Schocken Books, 1998.

Lit Like This: I discovered, after writing this poem (and after its publication in *Consonant Lights: an anthology of poems*), that the closing couplet is similar to the last line in Anne Sexton's poem, "The Poet of Ignorance" (from *The Paris Review*, issue no. 69, Winter 1974), featured in *Paris Review Poetry* online, August 27, 2022; a discovery that brought a flutter of discomfort.

The Way She Worked: An earlier version of this poem was written for *Magical Carpets*— a 12" x 10" watercolour and ink painting by Women's Art Association of Canada studio artist, Barbara Feith (1927-2021), for an exhibition and reading celebrating National Poetry Month in 2018.

Corroborate the Audio: "*die böhmische Seite des Berges*" translates: "the Bohemian side of the mountain."

Catalytic: The incident of the deaths of Nadav and Avihu on the day of the consecration of the mishkan (tent of meeting) is related briefly in Leviticus 10:1-2. In *The Stone Edition Torah*, the verses are translated: "The sons of Aaron, Nadab and Avihu, each took his fire pan, they put fire in them and placed incense upon it; and they brought before HASHEM [God] an alien fire that He had not commanded them. A fire came forth from before HASHEM [from the space between the cherubs' faces and wings on the holy ark] and consumed them, and they died before HASHEM."

Beam Me Up: The first stanza was composed from notes I took while listening to author Souvankham Thammavongsa, guest editor of *Best Canadian Poetry* 2021, in conversation with Anita Lahey for the Zoom launch of the anthology; November 10, 2021.

Stuff That Stirs: *Encre sympathique* (Gallimard, 2019)—the "recent book" by Patrick Modiano. Translated *Invisible Ink* by Mark Polizzotti, Yale University Press, 2020.

Spectral: Written in response to pinhole photographer Jan Hinderson's luminous pinhole photo, featured in *Pinhole Poetry*, issue 2.3, October 2023.

Larkspurs: 'Blacknights' are a deep black-purple strain of hollyhock. 'Galahads', also called candle larkspur, are towering perennials that feature spikes of white flowers. This poem owes a debt of gratitude to Mark Strand's poem, "Giving Myself Up," from his 1970 collection, *Darker; Collected Poems*, Alfred A. Knopf, 2014.

Acknowledgements

Sincere thanks to the publishers and editors of the publications in which poems in this collection first appeared, many in earlier renditions; thanks to the judges and jurors who nominated and/or selected some of these poems for awards:

acta victoriana: "Spruce"
Anacapa Review: "Juney, It's You"
The Antigonish Review: "Why Verify That Rain"
Arc Poetry Magazine: "Use of the Room"—Award of Awesomeness, September 2021; "Porthole to the Shades"—Award of Awesomeness, Honourable Mention, October 2022; "Larkspurs"
Asemana Magazine: "Refinement"; "Screwdriver"
Bear Review: "O-zone"
Blood + Honey: "Behemoth of the Salt Lick"; "Listening to Philip Glass, Violin Concerto No.1"; "Stuff That Stirs"; "In Winnipeg on the Centenary of Kafka's Death"
Consonant Lights: an anthology of poems: "Lit Like This"; "Garden Yellows"
Contemporary Verse 2: "Descant"
DUSIE Tuesday Poem #564: "Impromptu with an Emptying Pen"
FreeFall Magazine: "After-cast"
Grain: the journal of eclectic writing: "Sun Colours, Deep Field"—Second Place, 2021 Short Grain Contest
Horseshoe Literary Magazine: "Cherry Compote"
Juniper: "Canterbury Bells"
League of Canadian Poets Poetry Pause: "Manu's sphere"; "Winter Work"; "Noon"; "Luna"
The Mantle: "Ice-lace"; nominated for a 2022 Pushcart Prize
Montréal Serai: "Concertina"; "Forty Years"; "Porthole to the Shades"; "Knocking the Next"; "At the Heart of the Ghost"
The Nashwaak Review: "Winter Work"; "Sleight"; "Gmünd, 1920 / 2019"; "Gods of August"; "Corroborate the Audio"; "Infinity-love"
The Nelligan Review: "Luna"; "Docent"; "Three-prong Plugs Have Grounding Pins"; "These Snippets Lustrous & Doubled"
The New Quarterly: "Adept"—Honourable Mention, 2022 Nick Blatchford Occasional Verse Contest

Pinhole Poetry: "One Act with the Night Wolf"; included the inaugural Pinhole Press chapbook, 2022 Pinhole Poetry Selected and nominated for Best of the Net Anthology 2023; "Spectral"; "Or Else"; "Don't We Look Marvellous"

Poem Alone: "Sea Level"

Prairie Fire: "Kangaroo"; "Loquats"

Rat's Ass Review: "Fishing with DB"

Spring Pulse Poetry Festival: Dr. William Henry Drummond Poetry Anthology 2022: "Touch-No-Matter-What"

talking about strawberries all of the time: "Restless"; "When It Comes"

The /tEmz/ Review: "Gloss"; "Beam Me Up;" "What Now"; "Light from Water Where We Bothered It"

Train: a poetry journal: "Low under indigo"

Verse-Virtual: "Entering the painter's space"; "The Way She Worked"; "Dear Frankie on Falster"; "Craning for That Port"

Voices Israel Anthology 2024: "Catalytic"—Honourable Mention, Reuben Rose Competition; "Kangaroony"

Voices Israel Anthology 2025: "Bright Blue Stars"

yolk.: "Throwback"

Warm thanks to Sandra Barry for her careful reading and insightful feedback on a close-to-final draft of this collection, for granting permission to quote from her unpublished poem "Perigee Moon" in the opening epigraph, and for her kind and incisive back cover words.

Thanks to Ruth Panofsky and B.W. Powe for their discerning and gracious back cover words.

Thanks to Carmelo Militano for reading a close-to-final draft of this collection, for providing shrewd and unusual feedback, including back cover words.

Thanks to Jason Heroux for his enthusiastic permission to quote from his collection of magical prose poems, *Like a Trophy from the Sun* (Guernica Editions, 2024), in an opening epigraph.

Thanks to photographer Brenda Barry for the 'stick moon'

image that graces the cover spread of this book.

I am fortunate to count as friends and colleagues in the longstanding Long Dash group: John Oughton, Mary Lou Soutar-Hynes, Sheila Stewart, Clara Blackwood, Merle Nudelman, Brenda Clews, and Kath MacLean. Our regular meetings and readings over the years have been indispensable to the development of my writing and to my experience of literary community. Thank you, Long Dash!

Huge thanks to Guernica Editions for their dedication to authors and literature in Canada and internationally, and for their enduring faith in my work. It is an honour and a privilege to be published by GE: Connie Guzzo McParland, president; Michael Mirolla, vice-president and editor-in-chief; Anna van Valkenburg, associate publisher. Thanks to Errol F. Richardson, designer, and to Marisa Jorgensen and Crystal Fletcher, publicists, for rounding out the exceptional GE team.

Deep gratitude to my family, especially my life partner, Menachem Wolff.

About the Author

Elana Wolff is the author of eight solo collections of poetry, several collaborative works, a collection of essays on poems, and an original translation of poems from the Hebrew by Georg Mordechai Langer, co-translated with Menachem Wolff. Elana's poems and creative nonfiction pieces have appeared in publications in Canada and internationally and have garnered various awards. She has taught English for Academic Purposes at York University in Toronto and at The Hebrew University in Jerusalem, and currently divides her professional time between writing, literary editing, and designing and facilitating social and biographical art processes. Elana has twice won the Canadian Jewish Literary Award, in 2020 for her poetry collection, *Swoon*, and in 2024 for her cross-genre Kafka-quest work, *Faithfully Seeking Franz*, in the category of Jewish Thought and Culture.

ALSO BY ELANA WOLFF

POETRY:

Birdheart (Guernica Editions, 2001)
Mask (Guernica Editions, 2003)
You Speak to Me in Trees (Guernica Editions, 2006); recipient of the 2008 F.G. Bressani Prize; short-listed for the 2007 Acorn-Plantos Award for People's Poetry
Startled Night (Guernica Editions, 2011); long-listed for the ReLit Award
Helleborus & Allchémille (Éditions du Noroît, 2013); bilingual editions of poems selected from *Birdheart, Mask, You Speak to Me in Trees*, and *Startled Night*; French translation by Stéphanie Roesler awarded the 2014 John Glassco Prize in Literary Translation
Everything Reminds You of Something Else (Guernica Editions, 2017)
Swoon (Guernica Editions, 2020); recipient of the 2020 Canadian Jewish Literary Award for Poetry
Shape Taking (Ekstasis Editions, 2021)

ESSAYS:

Implicate Me: Short Essays on Contemporary Poems; introduction by Ellen S. Jaffe (Guernica Editions, 2010)

CREATIVE NONFICTION:

Faithfully Seeking Franz (Guernica Editions, 2023); recipient of the 2024 Canadian Jewish Literary Award in the category of Jewish Thought and Culture

CO-AUTHORED:

Slow Dancing: Creativity and Illness (Rengas and Duologue), with Malca Litovitz (Guernica Editions, 2008)
You Will Still Have Birds: a conversation in poems, with Susie Petersiel Berg (Lyricalmyrical, limited edition handmade chapbook, 2015)
Songs and Poems of Love by Georg Mordechai Langer, original

translation from the Hebrew, with Menachem Wolff; a flipside book including *A Hunger Artist & Others Stories* by Franz Kafka, translation by Thor Polson (Guernica Editions, 2014; second printing, 2015)

CO-EDITED:

Poet to Poet: Poems written to poets and the stories that inspired them; with Julie Roorda. (Guernica Editions, 2012)

A Disciplined Passion: Essays on the Works of Keith Garebian; with David Bateman and as contributors (Guernica Editions, 2025)

Printed by Imprimerie Gauvin
Gatineau, Québec